THE LITTLE
BOOK FOR
COCKTAIL
LOVERS

An Hachette UK Company
www.hachette.co.uk

Summersdale Publishers Ltd
Part of Octopus Publishing Group Limited
Carmelite House
50 Victoria Embankment
LONDON
EC4Y 0DZ
UK

www.summersdale.com

Printed and bound in Poland

ISBN: 978-1-80007-983-0

Substantial discounts on bulk quantities of Summersdale books are available to corporations, professional associations and other organizations. For details contact general enquiries: telephone: +44 (0) 1243 771107 or email: enquiries@summersdale.com.

Disclaimer
Neither the author nor the publisher can be held responsible for any loss or claim arising out of the use, or misuse, of the suggestions made herein. The publisher urges care and caution in the pursuit of any of the activities represented in this book. This book is intended for use by adults only. Please drink responsibly.

THE LITTLE BOOK FOR COCKTAIL LOVERS

RUFUS CAVENDISH

summersdale

CONTENTS

Introduction
6

Cocktail-Making Must-Haves
9

Learning the Lingo
19

Get Crafty
26

The Recipes
37

Last Word
126

Cocktail Index
127

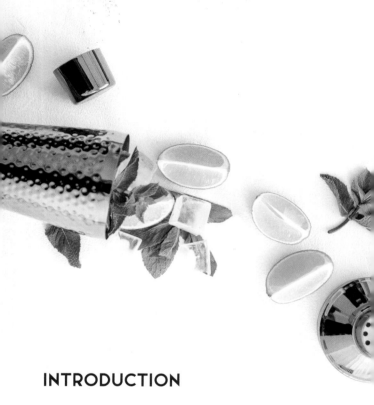

INTRODUCTION

Cocktail making – otherwise known as mixology – is part art and part science. It isn't a new concept: the creation of alcoholic beverages can be traced back to ancient history, and the time of medicine and magic – and perhaps this means mixology is part magic, too?

Cocktail culture changes depending on your location – it has roots all around the world, from rum-soaked tiki cocktails of the Americas to European classics with years of tradition. Historical events have also had a large part to play in the development of the cocktail – the Prohibition in the 1920s forced the hand of many bartenders in the USA to create a whole new wave of concoctions, often to dilute the potent bootleg alcohol. And now, looking toward the future, dozens of new cocktails are debuted at competitions yearly.

When making a cocktail, not only are you creating an object of artistry, but you're also producing something that can satisfy and satiate. There is a whole raft of reasons for creating a cocktail – be it to fulfil a personal craving or for it to be the centre of a social situation – but, whatever the purpose, one thing is for sure: cocktails belong as much to the lover of fine ingredients and quiet enjoyment, as they do to the high-spirited who love to be at the centre of a social whirlwind.

This book will provide all the know-how to start or continue on your cocktail journey. Read on to get to grips with the cocktail lingo, learn the tricks of the trade and master over 50 recipes.

So, let us raise our glass to cocktails: the conversation starters, the dance-floor encouragers and relationship instigators.

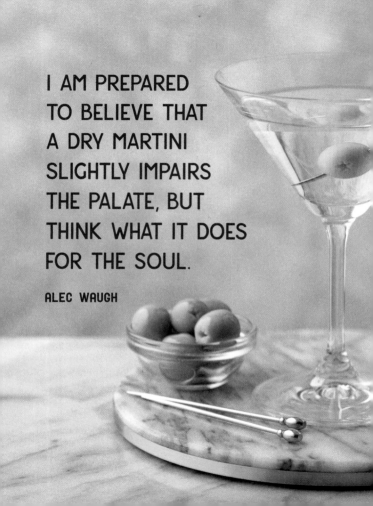

I AM PREPARED
TO BELIEVE THAT
A DRY MARTINI
SLIGHTLY IMPAIRS
THE PALATE, BUT
THINK WHAT IT DOES
FOR THE SOUL.

ALEC WAUGH

COCKTAIL-MAKING MUST-HAVES

When it comes to cocktail making,
you can go far with only a handful of
ingredients. The more you get creating,
the more you will discover the impact
that using the correct appliances
and ingredients can have on your
concoctions, although many can be
substituted with common kitchen items.

Essential Equipment

Cocktail shaker – Cocktail shakers are two-part contraptions, usually made of metal, that allow you to combine ingredients quickly and efficiently. There are several different varieties, each with their own advantages, but beginners don't need to worry. Cocktail shakers can be substituted by placing a large metal or plastic cup upside down in a pint glass to form a secure chamber (if they get stuck together after shaking, knock the side of the metal cup with the flat of your hand).

Jug – A jug is a jug! Some cocktails – especially sharing ones – need to be prepared in a jug instead of a shaker. You can use any jug at hand, just make sure you check the capacity against the requirements of the recipe.

Strainer – Strainers are used to separate ice from the cocktail mix after shaking. Fine-mesh strainers are used when the cocktail contains solid ingredients, such as fruits, that may need to be worked through for final presentation. A common kitchen sieve works well for both purposes. Some cocktail shakers are designed with built-in strainers, but you can also buy them separately.

Bar spoon – A long-handled spoon designed to reach the bottom of a cocktail shaker or tall glass. A chopstick is a good replacement for stirring, but if pouring over (see page 22), use the back of a metal spoon.

Muddler – A heavy mixing rod with a weighted end to crush solid ingredients. The muddler is commonly used in recipes containing sugar, fruit and fragrant herbs. Some bar spoons have a built-in muddler at the end. A variety of kitchen items can be used in place of the muddler, but ideally you want something, such as a large wooden spoon, which will reach the bottom of what you are mixing your cocktail in.

Jigger – A jigger is a double-ended shot measurer. One end measures a single shot and the other a double shot. The standard measurement for a single and double changes around the world, although generally the former tends to be between 25 ml (⁴/₅ fl oz) and 45 ml (1 ³/₅ fl oz). Most jiggers have the measurement inscribed. A kitchen measuring jug usually starts at around 50 ml (1 ¾ fl oz) so won't be a good substitute – instead, try a shot glass.

Glasses

Choosing the right glass can really elevate the look of your cocktail. It acts as a shorthand, signalling to the drinker the experience they can expect. There are also practical concerns when choosing which glass to use. Short cocktails that focus on the spirit and liqueurs, and don't play too hard with distracting juices and syrups, generally require smaller glasses. On the other hand, long cocktails, such as slings and punches, are refreshing, deep drinks that are as much about the interaction of juice and spirit as the hit of alcohol, and they work best in taller glasses.

Here are the most common varieties of cocktail glass:

 Martini – Long-stemmed and wide-bowled, traditionally angular. The capacity of a standard Martini glass is typically around 120 ml (4 fl oz) to 250 ml (9 fl oz); used for short cocktails.

 Hurricane – A deep, bell-shaped glass. The largest of the common cocktail glasses, clocking in around 440 ml (15 fl oz). Perfect for long drinks.

 Highball – Also known as a collins glass, the highball is slimmer and taller than an old-fashioned. It can hold up to 300 ml (10 fl oz) and is used for long drinks.

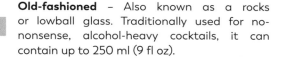

Old-fashioned – Also known as a rocks or lowball glass. Traditionally used for no-nonsense, alcohol-heavy cocktails, it can contain up to 250 ml (9 fl oz).

Flute – A tall-stemmed glass generally used for sparkling drinks. Recent generations have seen them replace coupe glasses as the champagne vessel of choice. A standard flute has a capacity of approximately 180 ml (6 fl oz).

Margarita – A long-stemmed, double-welled glass usually reserved for the Margarita family of drinks, although it took a brief side job in the 1970s to host prawn cocktails. It generally has a capacity of around 260 ml (9 fl oz).

Coupe – The original, but now out of fashion, champagne "saucer" is making a revival as a stylish all-purpose vessel for short cocktails. It has a capacity of around 180 ml (6 fl oz).

Mason jar – Are mason jars a fad or are they here to stay? These homey, folksy alternatives to highball and hurricane glasses have a great capacity, with some allowing for up to 630 ml (22 fl oz).

Garnishes

Garnishes are little enhancements that can add to the flavour and complement the cocktail design. Popular garnishes include the following:

A slice – Citrus fruits, sliced in rounds or half-rounds, provide an easy visual lift to any drink. Cut a slit in the slice and slide onto the rim of the glass for more impact.

A twist – The next step in citrus garnishes. Slice a round of citrus fruit, cut away the flesh and trim the peel to leave the thin outside skin strip; then twist the remaining peel by hand.

Herbs – Mint is a popular garnish and is even the key ingredient in well-known cocktails such as the Mojito. Other popular herbs used in cocktails include basil and rosemary.

Little bites – Little nibbles, such as maraschino cherries, olives or cocktail onions, can be skewered on a cocktail stick or dropped directly into the drink.

Flavoured rims – Margaritas are famous for the salty rim, created by dipping the rim of the glass in a liquid (water or lemon juice work well) and rolling in salt. Flavoured rims can come in all varieties, from sugars and spices to crazy popping candy.

Syrups and Bitters

Many believe a cocktail's best friend is a fine syrup or bitter, as they add dimension through flavour and colour.

Simple syrup – Simple syrup is the most commonly used type of syrup in cocktail making. It's made with a 1:1 ratio of sugar and water. It's easy to prepare at home and can be stored for up to three or four weeks in the fridge, when bottled hygienically.

Infused syrups – Once you've perfected a simple syrup, it's easy to level up to infused syrups. Adding bundles of herbs or stick spices, such as cinnamon, while the syrup heats helps to infuse the syrup with that flavour. Remember to strain before bottling so you don't have bits floating around in your drink!

Cocktail syrups – Cocktail syrups are pre-prepared infused syrups. Flavours include a range of fruits, nuts, herbs and spices, and caramels.

Bitters – Bitters are a type of spirit, often infused with botanicals, commonly used in cocktails such as Manhattans and Diplomats. Seeing as they are alcohols – and high-proof (strongly alcoholic) ones at that – they are used in such small quantities that their contribution to the alcohol content of your cocktail is negligible.

Alcohols

Cocktails are all about balance and harmony. Learn all the notes – in this case the different alcohols – and you'll soon be able to write the perfect cocktail symphony.

Spirit – Spirits are distilled alcohols. They are the most common alcoholic ingredient found in cocktails. They include whisky, rum, vodka, gin, tequila and more.

Liqueur – Liqueurs are distilled spirits. They generally have a lower proof (contain less alcohol) than spirits, as they are sweetened and may contain additional flavourings. Liqueurs popularly used in cocktail making include Angostura bitters, amaretto and limoncello.

Crème liqueur – Crème liqueurs are made from spirits but contain more sugar than liqueurs and, because of this, generally have a thicker, more syrupy texture. They can be flavoured with fruits, nuts or herbs and can be clear or colourful. Popular flavours include crème de menthe, crème de cassis and crème de cacao.

Cream liqueur – Cream liqueurs contain dairy products, such as cream, and a flavourful liqueur. Among the most famous are Irish cream liqueurs, which contain Irish whiskey, but others involve distilled rum, tequila, vodka and more. They are commonly sweet. Popular flavourings include coffee, chocolate, toffee, caramel and hazelnut. They are usually lower-proof alcohols.

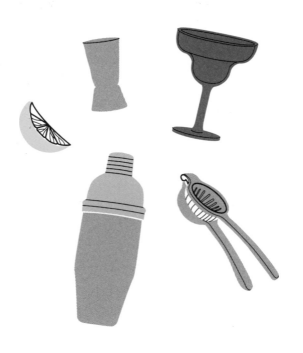

WHY LIMIT HAPPY
TO JUST AN HOUR?

LEARNING THE LINGO

From muddle to mix, and liqueur to layer, read on for an A–Z of the most commonly used terms in the cocktail-making sphere.

For all the over-the-shoulder cocktail shaking and pouring from a height that comes with flair bartending, cocktail making at its heart is quite simple. Most cocktails are created using the same few steps. Once you learn the language and have mastered the actions, you'll have an entire world of cocktail crafting at your fingertips!

Bruise

Cocktail recipes containing whole herbs, especially fragile ones such as basil, may ask you to bruise the plant. This releases the aromas and flavours of the herb that will then mingle with the liquids of the cocktail. Bruising can be achieved by muddling (see page 21) the herb into the drink but some aficionados prefer to avoid this, as they feel that too much damage to the leaf compromises the flavour. Instead, some choose to lightly smack the plant against the flat of their hand, before adding to the drink.

Dash

Terms such as dash or glug show up a lot in cooking and mixology, which can be very frustrating for the perfectionists and quantifiers among us. A dash can be different for everyone. The first thing to consider when you encounter the word "dash" in a recipe is to think that less is more – too much of any flavour would unbalance and overwhelm the other components. The second thing to consider is technique. If you're uncertain how much to use, try tilting the bottle and quickly whipping it upright as soon as the liquid comes out.

Layer

Some cocktails gain their attractive appearance from the striking layers that are created. Think of the famous Tequila Sunrise, where the base layer of red grenadine dawns into tequila-infused orange juice. The technique is also popularly used in the creation of shooters (a small alcoholic beverage often drunk in one go), such as Squashed Frogs, Slippery Nipples or Lemon Violet shooters. Layering calls for careful pouring, with no subsequent stirring or shaking.

Muddle

This means applying pressure and pummelling the ingredients of your cocktail using a heavy implement. The purpose is to mash or crush soft ingredients, such as fruit and herbs, and grind hard ones, such as sugar and ice.

Pour over

You may be asked to pour over when making a delicate cocktail, such as one that requires clear layers. Pouring over means to pour the liquid on to the back of a bar spoon held over the glass. If you don't have a bar spoon, a standard spoon will do. This diffuses the liquid, helping it to land over a wider area with less force. This is more likely to help the new addition to settle gently over the liquid already in the glass.

Shake

Is there a more common term in mixology? How do you know when to shake and when to stir? The purpose of shaking is to combine the ingredients and, when using ice, to cool them. Sometimes shaking can change the texture of a cocktail, such as when using egg white to create a creamy froth. Traditionally, the ingredients are combined, usually with ice, in a cocktail shaker, which is then closed. This is followed by giving several good, hard shakes (or as directed by the recipe) and then straining the liquid, so the concoction is chilled but not watered down by melting ice.

Stir

Books and films would have you believe that stirring or shaking is the biggest dilemma you'll have to face in mixology. That simply isn't true! The two are quite different techniques that are used for different liquids. Stirring comes into its own for fizzy beverages, such as champagne. Shaking would eliminate the gas and flatten the drink, thereby taking all the fun out of it!

Strain

The most common use of the strainer is to transfer the cocktail from the shaker to the glass, preventing any crushed or cracked ice from falling into the tasty concoction you have just created. You might also use it when preparing drinks with whole or chunky ingredients that have been used to infuse the liquid with flavour but should not appear in the final presentation.

IT'S NEVER TOO EARLY FOR A COCKTAIL.

Noël Coward

GET CRAFTY

Cocktail creation is a sensory craft, and visual impact plays a large part in the experience of presenting and consuming a cocktail. From the simple elegance of an Espresso Martini dotted with a pair of coffee beans, to the pageantry of cocktails that arrive at your table nestled in their own scene, caged in glass with smoking dry ice, the beauty of a cocktail starts in the visuals. Here are a few crafts that will help you to shape your own cocktail narrative and bring pizzazz to your mixology.

DRIED FRUIT SLICES

This is a simple elevation of the classic fruit slice. When properly prepared and stored correctly, they can be kept for up to a year (depending on the fruit).

Equipment:

- Oranges, limes or lemons
- Chopping board
- Knife
- Kitchen roll
- Oven tray
- Greaseproof paper
- Large airtight jar

Method:

1. Choose your citrus of choice. The more vividly coloured the peel, the better the colour will preserve through the drying process.

2. Set oven to lowest possible setting.

3. Using the knife and the chopping board, slice into approximately 2 mm (1/8 in.) rounds.

4. Pat the rounds dry with kitchen roll and place them on greaseproof paper on a flat oven tray, making sure they are not overlapping.

5. Bake in the oven until they are dry – this can take a variable amount of time, although expect around 4–5 hours. Check regularly to ensure no rounds are burning.

6. When fully cooled and dried, transfer to an airtight jar.

DIY GLASS CHARMS

Personalize your glass with these DIY charms and make sure it never gets picked up by the wrong person when the drinks are flowing. Wine glass charm rings come ready-made and are widely (and inexpensively) available from online stores and general hobby stores, so this is a very quick and easy craft that's all about personal style.

Equipment:

- Six silver-plated wine glass charm rings
- Selection of six or more small beads

Method:

1. Select as many rings as you require.
2. Bead choice is the key to creating cocktail charms that reflect your, and your guests', personality. There is a wide selection available at many stores, from quirky fruits beads and vintage glass gems to chic charms. The ideal bead or charm is eye-catching and small enough to sit comfortably on the base of the glass.
3. Thread your beads onto each wine glass charm ring, making sure every design is different so no drink mix-ups will occur.
4. Serve plentiful cocktails at your latest soirée, secure in the knowledge that your drink won't be accidentally poached.

DISCO BALL DECORATIONS

Jazz up any drinks soirée with these handmade disco ball drink decorations. The 1970s-inspired disco-ball drinks toppers bring kitschy flair to any cocktail presentation. Pair with colourful concoctions to create a far-out ambience.

Equipment:

- Ping-pong ball
- Metal skewer
- 10 mm (³/₈ in.) square mirror mosaic tiles
- Glue
- Cocktail sticks/ toothpicks

Method:

1. Pierce the ping-pong ball – very carefully! – using the skewer to make a small hole to fit a cocktail stick/toothpick.
2. Glue each mosaic tile onto the ball (without covering the hole) and leave to dry.
3. Once dry, fit the ball onto the end of the cocktail stick/toothpick and fix in place with glue to secure properly. Leave for several hours to dry.
4. Serve with a frozen Margarita – and keep it frosty.

DÉCOUPAGE TRAY

Arrange your cocktails on this eye-catching tray for a real crowd pleaser.

Equipment:

- Découpage paper
- Découpage all-in-one glue and sealant
- Flat drinks tray – can be any material, as long as it's durable
- Ruler
- Scissors
- Brush or small silicone spatula
- Varnish

Method:

1. Take a moment to decide how you want your tray to look. You could use one colour or create a patchwork effect.
2. Measure the area you are covering and cut the découpage paper to the perfect size.
3. Cover the area you are papering with a thick layer of all-in-one glue and sealant. If you are using strips or patches, do this in sections.
4. Gently lay the paper over the glue and, with your brush, push out any wrinkles that have appeared.
5. Cover with several layers of all-in-one glue and sealant and leave to dry. Apply a layer of varnish to protect your design from spilled drinks.

FRUIT SKEWERS

One way to make an impact with your cocktail is to pile on the garnishes. Don't stop at a few slices on your glass, bring on the oversized fruit skewers!

Equipment:

- Wooden skewers
- Scissors
- Variety of bright and tropical fruits
- Knife
- Chopping board
- Bowl (optional)
- Spirit of your choosing (optional)

Method:

1. Cut your skewers down to the size of your choosing. Your fruit skewer should be longer than your glass by approximately a third.

2. Select fruits that complement the flavours of your planned cocktail.

3. Use the knife and chopping board to cut large- and medium-sized fruits into chunks. But be careful: too large and the fruit will be too heavy and slide down the skewer.

4. Optional – submerge the fruit into a bowl filled with a spirit of your choice. Cover and leave for an hour.

5. Drain and retain the alcohol. As a bonus, the spirit will be infused with the flavour of the fruit it covered.

6. Now the fun bit: slide the fruit onto the skewers.

FUN 'N' FRUITY PAPER DECORATIONS

These brightly coloured decorations are an inexpensive craft that creates impactful results. You can match your design to the ingredients in your cocktail – just make sure the fruit you use is symmetrical or it won't work.

Equipment:

- Long cocktail sticks/ toothpicks
- Scissors
- Brightly coloured craft paper

- Pen or pencil
- Ruler
- Glue

Method:

1. Cut a cocktail stick/toothpick to size to fit your glass of choice.

2. Draw and cut a fruit shape from your craft paper. This will be your template. The size should be approximately a quarter of the length of your cocktail stick/toothpick.

3. Cut around the template until you have 20–30 fruit shapes.

4. When you have the correct quantity of fruit shapes, fold each one in half lengthways.

5. Cover one half of your fruit shape in glue and stick to the side of one of the other cut-out fruit shapes, so that they open in the same direction. Repeat until you have made a little "book" of fruit shapes.

6. Leave to dry.

7. Stick the "front cover" and the "back cover" of the fruit-shaped book together, creating a 3D fruit.

8. Cover the tip of one cocktail stick in glue, insert it through the centre of the shape and leave to dry.

9. Once dry, fluff up your shape by running your finger around the leaves of the fruit and separating them as equally as possible.

MY FAVOURITE COCKTAIL IS THE ONE IN MY HAND

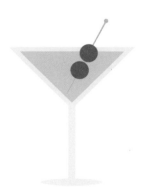

THE RECIPES

Now, the real fun begins!
From timeless classics to modern
favourites, in this section there is a
cocktail for every palate and occasion!
Unless specified, every recipe serves
one, so if you're sharing with others,
you'll need to adjust the ingredients!

So, what are you waiting for?
Dive in and start creating!

HONEY BEE

Sweet, sharp and a little unexpected, this is a modern cocktail with a sting in its tail.

Equipment:

- Cocktail shaker, with ice to add
- Bar spoon
- Strainer
- Martini glass

Ingredients:

- ½ tbsp (⅓ fl oz) runny honey
- 15 ml (½ fl oz) slightly cooled boiled water
- 60 ml (2 fl oz) white rum
- 40 ml (1 ⅖ fl oz) lemon juice
- Handful of ice (optional)
- Lemon peel, for garnish

Method:

1. Add the honey and warm boiled water to the cocktail shaker and stir until the honey has dissolved.

2. Add the rum and stir again.

3. Add the lemon juice and the ice.

4. Shake until combined and chilled.

5. Strain into the Martini glass, over ice if you prefer it extra cold.

6. Serve with a twist of lemon peel.

DIRTY BANANA

The perfect cocktail for milkshake lovers – or anyone who wants to try a new take on a tropical flavour.

Equipment:

- Blender, filled with two handfuls of crushed ice
- Hurricane glass

Ingredients:

- 1 overripe banana
- 60 ml (2 fl oz) white rum
- 30 ml (1 fl oz) coffee liqueur
- 30 ml (1 fl oz) crème de banane
- 30 ml (1 fl oz) crème de cacao (optional)
- 60 ml (2 fl oz) single cream or coconut cream

Method:

1. Peel the banana and break it into chunks. Optional – before you do this, slice off the tip with its peel on and retain for a garnish.
2. Blend the banana and all of the remaining ingredients with the crushed ice. For some drama, hold back the coffee liqueur and pour it over the cocktail once transferred to the glass. This will filter down in dark rolling clouds.
3. Pour into the hurricane glass.

FUZZY NAVEL

A Fuzzy Navel may not sound appealing but when you learn how simple it is to prepare, and how sweet and tangy it tastes, you won't be able to resist it. One of the gentler recipes in this book, it's a great pick for when you want to enjoy yourself in moderation. However, if you are looking for something stronger, add 30 ml (1 fl oz) of vodka at the start to transform your Fuzzy Navel into a Hairy Navel!

Equipment:

- Cocktail shaker, filled with ice
- Strainer
- Highball glass, filled with ice

Ingredients:

- 60 ml (2 fl oz) peach schnapps
- 140 ml (5 fl oz) orange juice
- Orange slice, to garnish

Method:

1. Add the schnapps and orange juice to the cocktail shaker.
2. Shake until combined and chilled.
3. Strain into the highball glass.
4. Add a slice of orange to the rim of your glass.

THE MARTINI:
THE ONLY AMERICAN
INVENTION AS PERFECT
AS THE SONNET.

H. L. MENCKEN

ESPRESSO MARTINI

It's quite possible that the Espresso Martini has outstripped its ancestor, the classic Martini, in popularity. However, why make two titans of the genre compete when you could simply enjoy them both?

Equipment:

- Cocktail shaker, filled with ice
- Strainer
- Martini glass

Ingredients:

- 60 ml (2 fl oz) vodka
- 30 ml (1 fl oz) espresso coffee, cooled
- 15 ml (½ fl oz) coffee liqueur
- 15 ml (½ fl oz) simple syrup
- Coffee beans, to garnish
- Chocolate shavings, to garnish (optional)

Method:

1. Add all the ingredients, except for the garnish, to the cocktail shaker.
2. Shake until combined and chilled.
3. Strain into the Martini glass.
4. Float the coffee beans on top for a finishing flourish. Sprinkle chocolate shavings over the serving if you have a sweet tooth.

COSMOPOLITAN

It is said that the Cosmopolitan is a descendent of the Daisy cocktail. It takes the pink of the Daisy and dials it up to 11 by using cranberry juice. This is quite a sharp cocktail and is best served – and consumed – while still ice cold.

Equipment:

- Cocktail shaker, filled with ice
- Strainer
- Martini glass, chilled

Ingredients:

- 30 ml (1 fl oz) vodka
- 30 ml (1 fl oz) triple sec
- 90 ml (3 fl oz) cranberry juice
- 30 ml (1 fl oz) lime juice
- Lime twist, to garnish

Method:

1. Add all of the ingredients, except for the garnish, to the cocktail shaker.
2. Shake until all the ingredients are combined and chilled.
3. Strain into the chilled Martini glass.
4. Garnish with a lime twist.

FUN FACTS

While no one knows when alcohol was first produced, artefacts have been found suggesting that fermented beverages were around from as early as the Neolithic era. Since then, humans have mixed alcohol with many ingredients – but with a very different purpose than making today's cocktails! Historically, doctors and apothecaries would infuse beers and wines with different ingredients to create cures for various ailments. The ancient Greek surgeon Antyllus suggested that a brew of beer mixed with crushed earthworms would aid milk production for breastfeeding women.

Medicine wasn't the only reason humans were mixing their drinks. In Homer's *Iliad*, women prepare a concoction designed to raise the spirits of down-on-their-luck soldiers. How would you like to try wine with grated strong goat's cheese (using a bronze grater, of course) and garnished with barley? It is still unclear whether this was a genuine contemporary recipe of Homer's or a fantastical invention to suit his larger-than-life warriors. After all, humans enjoy pairing cheese and wine to this day, although not often in the same glass.

LONG ISLAND ICED TEA

This menu fixture seems to take the straightforward booziness of classic cocktails and apply it to the heady "throw it all together" approach of modern mixology. Despite its scattered approach to spirits selection, you know where you are with a Long Island Iced Tea: drunk.

Equipment:

- Jug
- Bar spoon
- Highball glass, filled with ice

Ingredients:

- 15 ml (½ fl oz) tequila
- 15 ml (½ fl oz) vodka
- 15 ml (½ fl oz) triple sec
- 15 ml (½ fl oz) gin
- 15 ml (½ fl oz) rum
- 15 ml (½ fl oz) lemon or lime juice
- 20 ml (⅔ fl oz) simple syrup
- Cola, to top

Method:

1. Add all the ingredients, except the cola, into a jug and stir with a bar spoon until fully mixed.
2. Add the cola to the jug and gently stir with the bar spoon.
3. Pour into the highball glass.

MARGARITA

With its distinctive glass and salt rim, the Margarita is arguably one of the most renowned cocktails of all time.

Equipment:

- Plate, for the salt
- Margarita glass
- Cocktail shaker, filled with ice
- Strainer

Ingredients:

- Salt, for the rim of the glass
- 60 ml (2 fl oz) tequila
- 30 ml (1 fl oz) triple sec
- 30 ml (1 fl oz) lime juice
- Lime slice, to garnish

Method:

1. Cover a plate with salt. Dip the rim of the Margarita glass in water, or rub with a lime, and roll it in the salt. Leave to dry.
2. Add the tequila, triple sec and lime juice to the cocktail shaker.
3. Shake until all the ingredients are combined and chilled.
4. Strain into the Margarita glass.
5. Garnish with a lime slice.

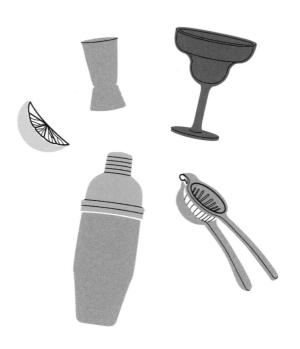

I TAKE LIFE WITH
A PINCH OF SALT,
A SQUEEZE OF LEMON
AND A MARGARITA

KIR ROYALE

The crème de cassis adds a little purple blush to the bottom of the champagne flute. Raspberry and orange liqueurs are other good additions for colour and flavour, depending on the notes of the champagne. The frozen berries add a sophisticated finish and have the added benefit of keeping your drink cool.

Equipment:

- Champagne flute

Ingredients:

- 15 ml (½ fl oz) crème de cassis
- Champagne, chilled, to top
- Frozen blackberries, to garnish

Method:

1. Add the crème de cassis to the flute.
2. Top with champagne.
3. Garnish with the frozen blackberries.

LEMON VIOLET SHOOTER

Whether you layer first the lemon cream liqueur and then the crème de violette, or vice versa, will depend on the proof of the liqueur you purchase. Because both are sweet concoctions, it's down to which has the higher alcohol content – the higher the proof, the lighter the drink. So check and make sure you put the heavier, lower-proof drink at the bottom. The order won't affect the flavour, just the appearance of the shooter. You may want to reserve a few portions for experimentation!

Equipment:

- Shooter glass
- Bar spoon

Ingredients:

- 30 ml (1 fl oz) lemon cream liqueur
- 30 ml (1 fl oz) crème de violette

Method:

1. Add your first alcohol to the shooter glass.
2. Using the bar spoon, carefully pour over the second liqueur.

NEGRONI

The Italian classic Negroni is a strong cocktail that may be too bitter for some tastes. However, for those who are tired of over-sweet modern confections, this is the classic alternative.

Equipment:

- Bar spoon
- Cocktail shaker, filled with ice
- Strainer
- Old-fashioned glass, filled with an oversized ice cube

Ingredients:

- 30 ml (1 fl oz) gin
- 30 ml (1 fl oz) sweet vermouth
- 30 ml (1 fl oz) Campari
- Orange peel, to garnish

Method:

1. Stir the liquid ingredients together in the cocktail shaker until combined and chilled.
2. Place an oversized ice cube in the old-fashioned glass.
3. Strain the cocktail into the glass.
4. Garnish with the orange peel.

DARK AND STORMY

The Dark and Stormy, like any other stir-in-the-glass cocktail, is excellent for any situation where you expect to be serving high quantities of people. Simple and easy prep means you can spend less time fussing with jiggers and muddlers, and more time raising a glass.

Equipment:

- Bar spoon
- Highball glass, half-filled with cracked ice

Ingredients:

- 120 ml (4 ⅕ fl oz) chilled ginger beer
- 30 ml (1 fl oz) lime juice
- 60 ml (2 fl oz) dark or spiced rum
- Lime wedge, to garnish

Method:

1. Add first the ginger beer and lime juice to the highball glass and gently stir.
2. Pour over the rum to create a dramatic layered effect.
3. Perch the lime wedge on the rim of the glass.
4. The flavours work really well when combined. If you prefer, add first the rum and lime juice, and then the ginger beer, and gently stir.

DIFFERENT COCKTAILS FOR DIFFERENT SATURDAY NIGHTS.

Drew Barrymore

LOTUS BLOSSOM

The Lotus Blossom appears to be quite a pretty cocktail but don't be fooled by its soft, cloudy appearance; the sake really lands a punch. Any sake works well but, for a touch of luxury, try a plum-infused sake to enjoy a sweeter and richer experience.

Equipment:

- Cocktail shaker, filled with ice
- Strainer
- Old-fashioned glass

Ingredients:

- 60 ml (2 fl oz) vodka
- 30 ml (1 fl oz) sake
- 60 ml (2 fl oz) lychee juice

Method:

1. Add the vodka, sake and lychee juice to the cocktail shaker and shake until combined.
2. Strain into the old-fashioned glass.

CLASSIC BOURBON SMASH

Smashes are cocktails that commonly start with fruit, herbs and ice muddled – smashed, if you will – in a cocktail shaker. This cocktail demonstrates the evergreen template of the smash which, once mastered, can form the basis of many delicious concoctions.

Equipment:

- Muddler
- Cocktail shaker, filled with ice
- Strainer
- Old-fashioned glass, filled with ice

Ingredients:

- 1 lemon, cut into 4 wedges , plus a slice to garnish
- 4 mint leaves, plus a sprig to garnish
- 60 ml (2 fl oz) bourbon
- 15 ml (½ fl oz) simple or maple syrup

Method

1. First, muddle the lemon wedges in the cocktail shaker, until the juices have been released.
2. Then muddle the mint, until bruised.
3. Add the liquid ingredients, shaking well to combine, before straining into the old-fashioned glass.
4. Garnish with a sprig of mint and a lemon slice.

CAIPIRINHA

Brazil's national cocktail is a simple mix of spirit, sugar and lime muddled together to make an outstanding combination. Traditionally, the cocktail is muddled in the glass but, depending on your bicep power, you may wish to pre-squeeze the lime into the glass to ensure you get as much juice as possible. It's cheating, but we won't tell!

Equipment:

- Old-fashioned glass, with crushed ice to be added
- Muddler
- Bar spoon

Ingredients:

- 1 lime, cut into wedges
- 2 tsp white fine sugar
- 60 ml (2 fl oz) cachaça
- Lime slice, to garnish

Method:

1. Add all ingredients to the glass and muddle together vigorously, until you're sure the lime has released its juice and the sugar is dissolved.
2. Fill the glass with ice and stir.
3. Garnish with the lime slice.

FUN FACTS

The Prohibition Era (1920–1933) was a 13-year period in the United States' history during which the sale, production and transportation of alcohol was forbidden. Although relatively brief, it has had a deep impact on American social and cultural history, contributing to the spread of jazz, the increased acceptability of women in bars and the image of early twentieth-century gangsters.

Most importantly for some, the Prohibition Era changed the face of cocktails forever! With the production and importation of alcohol banned, enterprising black marketeers distilled their own spirits to fill the gap. This alcohol, often known as moonshine, was produced using off-book contraptions and cheap ingredients. The result? Alcohol that was not delicious and only more or less drinkable.

Bootleggers, speakeasy barmen and the desperately thirsty mixed this DIY alcohol with powerful flavours designed to move the needle from less to more drinkable. For example, the Bee's Knees cocktail, invented in the mid-1920s, utilized honey and lemon to mask the distinctive flavour of "bathtub" gin.

BOURBON SOUR

Sours are often made using egg white so require a little extra oomph when working the cocktail shaker. The egg white contributes to the smooth, silky texture and signature white froth topping, but only if shaken with enough energy.

Equipment:

- Cocktail shaker, plus ice to add
- Strainer
- Coupe glass

Ingredients:

- 60 ml (2 fl oz) bourbon
- 20 ml (⅔ fl oz) lemon juice
- 15 ml (½ fl oz) simple syrup
- 15 ml (½ fl oz) egg white*

Method:

1. Add all the ingredients to the cocktail shaker.
2. Shake with gusto until the mixture is frothy.
3. Add the ice and shake again until chilled.
4. Strain into the coupe glass. If successful, the sour should have a layer of white froth on top.

* Consuming raw egg poses an increased risk of salmonella.

ORIGINAL PLANTER'S PUNCH

This drink is a thirst quencher, perfect for the Jamaican heat from where it is rumoured to originate.

Equipment:

- Cocktail shaker, filled with ice
- Strainer
- Highball glass, filled with ice

Ingredients:

- 90 ml (3 fl oz) dark rum
- 15 ml (½ fl oz) simple syrup
- 25 ml (⁴/₅ fl oz) lemon or lime juice
- 10 ml (¹/₃ fl oz) grenadine
- 2 dashes of Angostura bitters
- Soda water, to top
- Pinch of grated nutmeg, to garnish
- Sprig of mint, to garnish

Method:

1. Add all the ingredients, except the soda water and garnishes, to the cocktail shaker.
2. Shake vigorously to create the frothy top.
3. Strain into the highball glass.
4. Top with soda water.
5. Sprinkle the nutmeg on top of the cocktail and garnish with a sprig of mint.

AFTER ENOUGH GIMLETS I BECOME GIN-VINCIBLE

SQUASHED FROG

This long shot is much more mouth-watering than its name would indicate. The layers are very striking – just don't linger too long on comparing them to the unfortunate amphibian that gave it its name.

Equipment:

- Long shot glass
- Bar spoon

Ingredients:

- 15 ml (½ fl oz) grenadine syrup
- 15 ml (½ fl oz) melon liqueur
- 15 ml (½ fl oz) advocaat

Method:

1. To layer this drink, start by pouring grenadine into the bottom of the glass. As it has the highest sugar content and no alcohol, it is the heaviest, so works as a good bottom layer.

2. Using the back of the bar spoon, gently pour over the melon liqueur.

3. Using the back of your spoon, slowly add the advocaat for the top layer.

MOJITO

The Mojito is another cocktail that requires muddling. The key to this simple drink is the sugar, which helps to soften the impact of the alcohol.

Equipment:

- Cocktail shaker
- Muddler
- Strainer
- Highball glass, filled with ice
- Bar spoon

Ingredients:

- 1 lime, halved
- 4 mint leaves, plus a sprig for garnish
- 1 tsp of granulated sugar
- 60 ml (2 fl oz) white rum
- Soda water, to top

Method:

1. Remove the pips from the lime, and squeeze the juice over the mint leaves and sugar in the cocktail shaker.
2. Muddle until the mint leaves are bruised.
3. Strain the mixture into the highball glass.
4. Pour in the rum and gently stir together.
5. Top with soda water.

LIMONCELLO THYME

Thyme is a classic herb and it's so great to see it crop up more in the recent wave of botanical-inspired cocktails.

Equipment:

- Cocktail shaker, with ice to add
- Muddler
- Strainer
- Old-fashioned glass, filled with ice

Ingredients:

- 2 sprigs of thyme, plus one for garnish
- 60 ml (2 fl oz) gin
- 30 ml (1 fl oz) limoncello
- 30 ml (1 fl oz) lime juice, freshly squeezed
- Soda water, to top
- Lemon slices, for garnish

Method:

1. Muddle two sprigs of thyme in the cocktail shaker, then add the ice.
2. Pour in the gin, limoncello and lime juice, and shake thoroughly.
3. Strain into the old-fashioned glass and top with soda water.
4. Garnish with one sprig of thyme and lemon slices.

IF LIFE
GIVES YOU
LIMES, MAKE
MARGARITAS.

JIMMY BUFFETT

MINT JULEP

A julep is traditionally served in a small silver or pewter cup with no handle. It is thought that drinkers should hold the cup by the base or rim, allowing the ice inside the cup to seep into the metal and truly chill the beverage.

Equipment:

- Cocktail shaker, filled with ice
- Strainer
- Highball glass, filled with ice

Ingredients:

- 60 ml (2 fl oz) bourbon
- 10 mint leaves, plus a sprig to garnish
- 15 ml (½ fl oz) sugar syrup

Method:

1. Add the bourbon, mint and sugar syrup to the cocktail shaker.
2. Shake until combined and cooled.
3. Strain into the highball glass.
4. Add the sprig of mint to garnish.

FUN FACTS

Although the classics remain an evergreen playground for mixologists to both faithfully recreate and twist into new variations, there's plenty of room on the cocktail menu for new creations.

London bartender Dick Bradsell, a prolific cocktail maestro, flourished in the late twentieth century, whipping up a new generation of cocktails. One of his most famous creations, the Espresso Martini, was reportedly invented at the behest of a supermodel who requested a cocktail that would wake her up and keep the party going. Other cocktails of his creation include the Bramble, the Raspberry Martini, Russian Spring Punch and the playfully named Wibble.

CORPSE REVIVER NO.1

The term "corpse reviver" has been used since the mid-1800s to refer to strong cocktails that are supposedly able to cure a hangover, although it only became a cocktail in itself in 1930, in *The Savoy Cocktail Book*. The perfect drink for whenever you need a little back-to-life magic!

Equipment:

- Cocktail shaker, filled with ice
- Bar spoon
- Strainer
- Martini glass

Ingredients:

- 60 ml (2 fl oz) brandy
- 60 ml (2 fl oz) cognac
- 60 ml (2 fl oz) sweet vermouth

Method:

1. Stir together the ingredients in the cocktail shaker, until well chilled.
2. Strain into the Martini glass.

RAMOS GIN FIZZ

The Ramos Gin Fizz is a glass of frothy confection! The effect is assisted by adding a small quantity of single cream to the cocktail, resulting in a striking milky effect. Shaking this takes some gumption!

Equipment:

- Cocktail shaker, filled with ice
- Strainer
- Highball glass

Ingredients:

- 60 ml (2 fl oz) gin
- 15 ml (½ fl oz) lemon juice
- 15 ml (½ fl oz) lime juice
- 15 ml (½ fl oz) simple syrup
- 15 ml (½ fl oz) single cream
- 1 egg white*
- 3 dashes of orange blossom water
- Soda water, to top

Method:

1. Add all of the ingredients, except the soda water, to the cocktail shaker.
2. Shake until frothy – this can take up to 5 minutes!
3. Strain into the highball glass.
4. Top with soda water and enjoy.

* Consuming raw egg poses an increased risk of salmonella.

JERRY THOMAS'S WHISKEY COBBLER

Jerry Thomas did not claim to have invented the recipes in his bartender's guide, *The Bon Vivant's Companion* (1862), often considered the most influential cocktail tome in history. However, without knowing its true origin – and as this recipe is inspired by the one included in his signature volume – we'll dedicate this one to him.

In his original recipe, Jerry Thomas recommended using two wine glasses of whiskey, 1 tbsp sugar and two slices of orange. The traditionalists and the brave may like to observe the original ratios!

Equipment:

- Muddler
- Cocktail shaker, filled with ice
- Strainer
- Old-fashioned glass, filled with ice

Ingredients:

- 60 ml (2 fl oz) whiskey
- 1 tbsp of white fine sugar
- 1 orange, quartered, plus two slices to garnish

Method:

1. Muddle the whiskey, sugar and orange quarters in the cocktail shaker.
2. Strain the mixture into the old-fashioned glass over ice and top with two slices of orange, for garnish.

EL DIABLO

This cocktail may be named after the devil but its light, zingy flavours are as light as an angel's wing. The purple of the cocktail contrasts well with the green of the lime garnish, making the whole affair rather eye-catching.

Equipment:

- Cocktail shaker, filled with ice
- Strainer
- Highball glass, filled with ice

Ingredients:

- 60 ml (2 fl oz) tequila
- 20 ml (2/3 fl oz) crème de cassis
- 60 ml (2 fl oz) lime juice
- Ginger beer, to top
- Lime quarter, to garnish

Method:

1. Add all of the ingredients, except for the ginger beer and garnish, to the cocktail shaker.
2. Shake the mixture until fully combined and chilled.
3. Strain into the highball glass.
4. Gently top with ginger beer and garnish with the lime quarter.

INCOGNITO

It's the apricot brandy that is the star of the show here and gives it a touch of the winter warmer, even though the Incognito can be enjoyed year-round. What's incognito about this beverage? It could be that apricot brandy is rarely brandy at all – most apricot brandies are in fact apricot-flavoured liqueurs.

Equipment:

- Cocktail shaker, filled with ice
- Strainer
- Martini glass, chilled

Ingredients:

- 60 ml (2 fl oz) dry vermouth
- 60 ml (2 fl oz) cognac
- 40 ml (1 ⅖ fl oz) apricot brandy
- 3 dashes of Angostura bitters

Method:

1. Add all the ingredients to the cocktail shaker.
2. Shake until fully combined and chilled.
3. Strain into the chilled Martini glass.

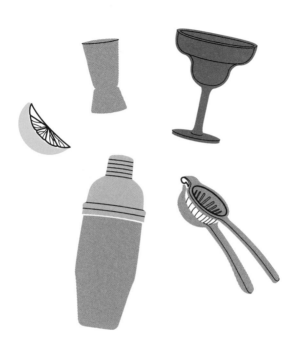

BLOODY MARY:
BRUNCH IN A GLASS

KNICKERBOCKER

Bright and sweet, this classic cocktail from the mid-1800s isn't as famous as some of its aged counterparts but when you taste it, you'll be surprised that it's fallen out of favour. Unlike the knee-length trousers from which it takes its name, the Knickerbocker deserves a revival!

Equipment:

- Cocktail shaker, filled with ice
- Strainer
- Old-fashioned glass, filled with crushed ice

Ingredients:

- 60 ml (2 fl oz) gold rum
- 15 ml (½ fl oz) orange curaçao
- 15 ml (½ fl oz) lime juice
- 15 ml (½ fl oz) raspberry syrup
- Fresh raspberries, to garnish
- Slice of lime, to garnish

Method:

1. Add all the ingredients, except for the garnish, to the cocktail shaker.
2. Shake well, until chilled and combined.
3. Strain into the old-fashioned glass.
4. Garnish with fresh raspberries and a slice of lime.

SLIPPERY NIPPLE

Sure, some cocktails are all about elegant surroundings, fine ingredients and harking back to the "good old days". But we shouldn't ignore mixology's fun, raunchier side. Slippery Nipples, Sex on the Beach and Pornstar Martinis – there's a lot to be said for the lighter side of cocktail culture!

Equipment:

- Long shot glass
- Bar spoon

Ingredients:

- 30 ml (1 fl oz) sambuca
- 30 ml (1 fl oz) Irish cream liqueur

Method:

1. Pour the sambuca into the long shot glass.
2. Using a bar spoon, carefully pour over the Irish cream liqueur to create two distinct layers.

MIDNIGHT STINGER

We tend to use the term "cocktail" as a catch-all for mixed beverages, but historically it has been used to define a drink served before dinner. The Midnight Stinger started life as a digestif – a drink served in the evening, after dinner – popular among the upper classes. Enjoy this cocktail whenever it takes your fancy!

Equipment:

- Cocktail shaker, filled with ice
- Strainer
- Old-fashioned glass, filled with crushed ice

Ingredients:

- 30 ml (1 fl oz) bourbon
- 30 ml (1 fl oz) Fernet liqueur
- 30 ml (1 fl oz) lemon juice
- Sprig of mint leaves, to garnish

Method:

1. Add all of the ingredients, except for the garnish, to the cocktail shaker.
2. Shake until fully combined and chilled.
3. Strain into the old-fashioned glass.
4. Lightly bruise the mint leaves and place on top as a garnish.

ENGLISH GARDEN

Like a traditional English garden, this cocktail is fresh,
verdant, slightly cloudy – and it features gin. It's a long
refreshing drink and doesn't need punching up, but you
could consider swapping out the elderflower cordial for
elderflower liqueur, if that's to your taste.

Equipment:

- Cocktail shaker,
  filled with ice
- Strainer
- Highball glass,
  filled with ice

Ingredients:

- 60 ml (2 fl oz) gin
- 75 ml (2 ³/₅ fl oz)
  cloudy apple juice
- 30 ml (1 fl oz)
  elderflower cordial
- 30 ml (1 fl oz) lime
  juice, freshly squeezed
- Handful of mint
  leaves, to garnish

Method:

1. Add all the ingredients, except for the garnish, to
   the cocktail shaker.
2. Shake until combined and chilled.
3. Strain into the highball glass.
4. Garnish with the mint leaves.

THERE COMES A TIME IN EVERY WOMAN'S LIFE WHEN THE ONLY THING THAT HELPS IS A GLASS OF CHAMPAGNE.

Bette Davis

PIÑA COLADA

Piña Coladas originate from Puerto Rico. There is much controversy over who created the infamous drink. Some stories attribute the recipe's invention to nineteenth-century Puerto Rican pirate Roberto Cofresí, although this version is highly disputed! Three different bartenders have claimed the recipe as theirs, but either way, Puerto Ricans clearly recognized the genius of the cocktail and adopted it as their official drink!

Equipment:

- Blender
- Hurricane glass, chilled

Ingredients:

- 60 ml (2 fl oz) coconut cream
- 60 ml (2 fl oz) pineapple juice
- 60 ml (2 fl oz) white rum
- Slice of pineapple, rind cut off
- Handful of ice
- A wedge of pineapple, to garnish

Method:

1. Blitz all the ingredients, except the garnish, in the blender on the highest speed until completely blended.

2. Pour into the chilled hurricane glass and garnish with a wedge of pineapple

ZOMBIE

The Zombie cocktail is from the tiki family of cocktails. While this recipe suggests using a hurricane glass, traditionally tiki cocktail culture is known for its fun and flamboyant drinks receptacles.

Equipment

- Cocktail shaker, filled with ice
- Strainer
- Hurricane glass, filled with ice

Ingredients:

- 30 ml (1 fl oz) dark rum
- 30 ml (1 fl oz) white rum
- 30 ml (1 fl oz) lime juice
- 30 ml (1 fl oz) lemon juice
- 120 ml (4 1/5 fl oz) pineapple juice
- 30 ml (1 fl oz) passion fruit syrup
- 10 ml (1/3 fl oz) grenadine
- Sprig of mint, to garnish

Method:

1. Add all of the ingredients, except the grenadine and garnish, to the cocktail shaker.
2. Shake until well combined and chilled.
3. Strain into the hurricane glass.
4. Carefully pour the grenadine into the top of the glass.
5. Garnish with a sprig of mint.

FUN FACTS

Tiki cocktails appropriate a Polynesian styling, but their origins are firmly American. The tiki craze first cropped up in the US in the 1930s and can largely be traced back to one man: Donn Beach. Like the cocktails he went on to invent, there was a certain amount of mythmaking to Donn. He was born Ernest Raymond Beaumont Gantt but later adopted the name of his Los Angeles bar, Donn Beachcombers. While Trader Vic is often credited with the invention of the Mai Tai, Donn Beach also lays claim to it. Other cocktails to Donn Beach's name include the Zombie, Tahitan Rum Punch and Navy Grog. The latter was said to be Frank Sinatra's favourite drink when he frequented Donn's establishments.

Hollywood celebrities and stars flocked to Donn Beach's bar, such as Bing Crosby, Charlie Chaplin and Marlene Dietrich – although Marlene in particular seems to be linked with every cocktail joint in the early twentieth century!

MAI TAI

While the Mai Tai works very well as a refreshing single-serving drink, this recipe can easily scaled up for parties. If you are creating a batch of Mai Tai, simply multiply the ingredients by the number of drinkers and mix in a jug filled with crushed ice.

Equipment:

- Cocktail shaker, filled with ice
- Strainer
- Old-fashioned glass, filled with ice

Ingredients:

- 30 ml (1 fl oz) dark rum
- 20 ml (⅔ fl oz) orange curaçao
- 15 ml (½ fl oz) almond syrup
- 30 ml (1 fl oz) lime juice
- 50 ml (1 ¾ fl oz) pineapple juice
- Maraschino cherry and a segment of pineapple, to garnish

Method:

1. Add all the ingredients, except the garnish, to the cocktail shaker.
2. Shake well until combined and chilled.
3. Strain into the old-fashioned glass.
4. Skewer the cherry and pineapple on a cocktail stick, and balance it on the rim.

THE LAST WORD

This cocktail was first introduced in Detroit, via the Detroit Athletic Club, just before the start of the Prohibition Era. It then fell out of favour, before being revived in the early twenty-first century in Seattle. It takes advantage of the herbal liqueur Chartreuse to create an unusual green hue that seems both deeply retro and ineffably modern.

Equipment:

- Cocktail shaker, filled with ice
- Strainer
- Coupe glass, chilled

Ingredients:

- 30 ml (1 fl oz) gin
- 30 ml (1 fl oz) green Chartreuse liqueur
- 30 ml (1 fl oz) maraschino liqueur
- 30 ml (1 fl oz) lime juice
- Maraschino cherry, to garnish

Method:

1. Add all the ingredients, except for the garnish, to the cocktail shaker.
2. Shake until combined and chilled.
3. Strain into the chilled coupe glass.
4. Garnish with maraschino cherry for a vivid contrast.

COCKTAILS AND ME, WE'RE MINT TO BE!

GIN DAISY

A Gin Daisy can be traced all the way back to Jerry Thomas's guide on how to mix cocktails, although it probably preceded even that. Its secret to longevity is that it's close to perfection: a little sour, a little sweet, with grown-up flavours and a delicate blush pink colour.

Equipment:

- Cocktail shaker, filled with ice
- Strainer
- Old-fashioned glass, filled with ice

Ingredients:

- 15 ml (½ fl oz) triple sec
- 15 ml (½ fl oz) grenadine
- 20 ml (²/₃ fl oz) lemon juice
- Soda water, to top

Method:

1. Add all the ingredients, except the soda water, to the cocktail shaker.
2. Shake until combined and cooled.
3. Strain into the old-fashioned glass and top with soda water.

KIWI COLLINS

For all that mixology is the playground of tropical fruits, it seems that the kiwi doesn't get much of a look-in – until now! With its soft flesh that muddles well and the light, zingy flavour that happily balances with many spirits, this is a classic in the making.

Equipment:

- Cocktail shaker, with ice to add
- Muddler
- Strainer
- Highball glass, filled with ice

Ingredients:

- 1 kiwi, peeled
- 60 ml (2 fl oz) vodka
- 40 ml (1 ²/₅ fl oz) lemon juice
- 15 ml (½ fl oz) simple syrup
- Soda water, to top
- Slice of kiwi, with peel removed, to garnish

Method:

1. Muddle the kiwi in the base of the cocktail shaker.
2. Add the ice, vodka, lemon juice and simple syrup.
3. Shake vigorously until combined.
4. Strain into the highball glass and top with soda water.
5. Garnish with the slice of kiwi.

AVIATION

Violet has fallen out of favour as a flavour – could now be the time to reconsider it? Its floral notes match well with the botanicals of the gin. Some modern recipes omit the crème de violette to suit current tastes, but it would be a shame to lose the stunning lilac shade and classic flavour profile.

Equipment:

- Cocktail shaker, filled with ice
- Strainer
- Coupe glass, chilled

Ingredients:

- 15 ml (½ fl oz) lemon juice
- 15 ml (½ fl oz) maraschino liqueur
- 15 ml (½ fl oz) crème de violette
- Lemon peel and cherries, to garnish

Method:

1. Add all the ingredients, except the garnish, to the cocktail shaker.
2. Shake until combined and cooled.
3. Strain into the chilled coupe glass.
4. Garnish with twisted lemon peel and cherries.

SPARKLING CITRUS PUNCH
Serves 20

This punch's base of champagne makes it a wonderful addition to any festivity.

Equipment:

- Saucepan
- Wooden spoon
- Punchbowl or jug, filled with ice
- Ladle
- Punch glasses

Ingredients:

- 120 ml (4 ⅕ fl oz) water
- 120 g (4 oz) sugar
- 4 sprigs of rosemary
- 750 ml (26 ⅖ fl oz) champagne
- 120 ml (4 ¼ fl oz) grapefruit juice
- 120 ml (4 ⅕ fl oz) orange juice
- 30 ml (1 fl oz) grenadine

Method:

1. Create a rosemary-infused sugar syrup by adding the water, sugar and rosemary to a saucepan, and bringing to the boil. Once brought to boiling, lower the heat and stir until the sugar has completely dissolved.

2. Leave to cool before continuing with the recipe.

3. Combine the rosemary-infused sugar syrup and all the remaining ingredients in the punchbowl, or jug, and stir with the ladle.

4. Ladle into punch glasses.

COME
QUICKLY,
I AM TASTING
THE STARS!

DOM PÉRIGNON

SUMMER CUP
Serves 4

This recipe is for sharing. Ideally, the fruit and liquid should pour in equal measure, but gravity doesn't always play fair. Weigh the odds in your favour by doubling the fruit quantity and lightly muddling it in individual glasses before pouring.

Equipment:

- Muddler
- Large jug
- Bar spoon
- Mason jars

Ingredients:

- ½ cucumber, sliced into rounds
- 5 strawberries, halved
- 2 oranges, cut into wedges
- Handful of mint leaves, bruised, plus some for garnish
- 250 ml (8 $^4/_5$ fl oz) gin-based fruit liqueur, like Pimm's No. 1
- 550 ml (19 $^1/_3$ fl oz) lemonade, chilled

Method:

1. Lightly muddle the cucumber, strawberries and oranges, mint and liqueur in the jug.
2. Top with the lemonade and stir.
3. Pour into a mason jar.
4. Garnish with mint.

DIPLOMAT

For a cocktail that's named for diplomacy, this is not a recipe that bothers playing both sides. There's no attempt to disguise that this is a cocktail that favours vermouth lovers only.

Equipment:

- Cocktail shaker, filled with ice
- Bar spoon
- Strainer
- Martini glass, chilled

Ingredients:

- 40 ml (1 ²/₅ fl oz) dry vermouth
- 40 ml (1 ²/₅ fl oz) sweet vermouth
- 1 dash of maraschino liqueur
- 2 dashes of Angostura bitters
- Twist of orange peel, to garnish

Method:

1. Add all the ingredients, except the garnish, to the cocktail shaker.

2. Gently stir the mixture. Do not shake – shaking the mixture can froth and cloud the vermouth – this cocktail looks most inviting in its original clear amber.

3. Strain into the chilled Martini glass and garnish with the twist of orange peel.

MANHATTAN

Created in and named after the most sophisticated borough in the Big Apple, the Manhattan is said to be one of the most harmonious cocktails for flavour, when perfected.

Equipment:

- Cocktail shaker, filled with ice
- Bar spoon
- Strainer
- Martini glass

Ingredients:

- 70 ml (2 ½ fl oz) whiskey (rye or bourbon)
- 35 ml (1 ¼ fl oz) sweet vermouth
- 2–3 dashes of Angostura bitters
- 1 cherry or small slice of lemon peel, to garnish

Method:

1. Pour the whiskey (rye is recommended, but bourbon is fine if preferred), vermouth and bitters into the cocktail shaker.
2. Stir lightly but thoroughly. Shaking will make the cocktail cloudy to the eye and oily to the taste.
3. Strain the drink into the Martini glass and garnish with a cherry or lemon peel.

SNOWBALL

This retro 1970s cocktail is a festive treat and looks the part, with its creamy hue, lacy top and Santa-red cherry garnish. The lime cordial cuts through the cream of the advocaat, saving it from being too overwhelming during a season of rich food and indulgence.

Equipment:

- Highball glass
- Bar spoon

Ingredients:

- 60 ml (2 fl oz) advocaat
- 15 ml (½ fl oz) lime cordial
- 60 ml (2 fl oz) lemonade, to top
- Maraschino cherry, on a cocktail stick, to serve

Method:

1. Pour first the advocaat and then the lime cordial into the highball glass.
2. Top with the lemonade, while stirring, until fully combined.
3. Balance the cocktail stick on the rim of the glass.

FROZEN WATERMELON MARGARITA

Frozen drinks are to be enjoyed on scorching afternoons or on a balmy evening, after a large meal. The Watermelon Margarita is a particularly summery addition. Create a traditional salt rim by dipping the glass in water and rolling it in salt for a light contrast to the sweetness.

Equipment:

- Blender
- Strainer
- Margarita glass, chilled

Ingredients:

- 200 g (7 oz) frozen watermelon, cubed
- 30 ml (1 fl oz) silver tequila
- 20 ml (²/₃ fl oz) triple sec
- 1 tbsp sugar
- ½ lime
- Sparkling water, to top
- Wedge of watermelon, to garnish

Method:

1. In the blender, blitz the frozen watermelon, tequila, triple sec, sugar and juice of half a lime.
2. Strain the mixture into the chilled Margarita glass.
3. Gently top with sparkling water and garnish with a wedge of watermelon.

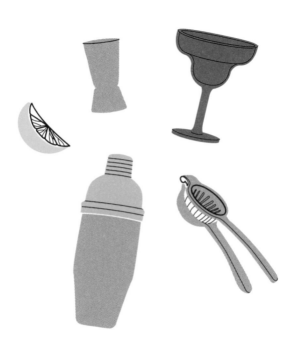

MAI-TAI OFFER
YOU A COCKTAIL?

NOBILE

This long cocktail is refreshing and – relatively – light on the alcohol. This makes it a good choice for sunny daytime drinking, or whenever you simply want to enjoy more than one beverage.

Equipment:

- Cocktail shaker, filled with ice
- Strainer
- Highball glass, filled with ice

Ingredients:

- 20 ml ($^2/_3$ fl oz) vodka
- 20 ml ($^2/_3$ fl oz) amaro
- Splash of limoncello
- 40 ml (1 $^2/_5$ fl oz) orange juice
- 40 ml (1 $^2/_5$ fl oz) apple and raspberry juice
- Bitter lemon, to top
- Sprig of mint, to garnish

Method:

1. Add all of the ingredients, except the bitter lemon and mint, to the cocktail shaker.
2. Shake until combined and chilled.
3. Strain into the highball glass.
4. Top with bitter lemon and garnish with the mint.

FRENCH 75

Known in France as Soixante Quinze, many believe that the French 75 is so named because it allegedly packs a similar punch to old 75 mm artillery guns. The simplicity of this recipe means that freshly squeezed lemon really does have an impact on the flavour profile so, if possible, choose fresh over bottled.

Equipment:

- Cocktail shaker, filled with ice
- Strainer
- Champagne flute

Ingredients:

- 60 ml (2 fl oz) gin
- 30 ml (1 fl oz) lemon juice
- 15 ml (½ fl oz) simple syrup
- Champagne, to top
- Lemon peel twist, to garnish

Method:

1. Add the gin, lemon juice and simple syrup to the cocktail shaker.
2. Shake until combined and chilled.
3. Strain into the champagne flute.
4. Top with champagne.
5. Garnish with the lemon peel.

APPLE PIE

This winter-warmer cocktail is perfect for drinking when wrapped up in front of the fire. If you don't fancy a hot drink, this cocktail works nearly as well cold, as the cinnamon whisky liqueur still provides a warming tingle.

Equipment:

- Highball glass
- Saucepan

Ingredients:

- 60 ml (2 fl oz) cinnamon whisky liqueur
- 60 ml (2 fl oz) vanilla vodka
- 120 ml (4 fl oz) cloudy apple juice
- Sliced dried apple, to serve

Method:

1. Combine the whisky liqueur and vodka directly in the highball glass.
2. Gently heat the apple juice in a saucepan, until warmed through.
3. Pour the warm apple juice over the alcohol.
4. Garnish with the sliced apple.

I COOK WITH WINE, SOMETIMES I EVEN ADD IT TO THE FOOD.

W. C. Fields

CHOCOLATE MUDSLIDE

This is one heavy cocktail! Milk or cream, chocolate sauce, cream liqueurs... It all adds up to a rich glass of indulgence.

Equipment:

- Cocktail shaker, with ice to add
- Strainer
- Highball glass

Ingredients:

- 30 ml (1 fl oz) coffee liqueur
- 30 ml (1 fl oz) Irish cream liqueur
- 30 ml (1 fl oz) vodka
- 60 ml (2 fl oz) milk or double/heavy cream
- 1 tsp chocolate sauce
- Chocolate sauce, to garnish
- Chocolate chips, to garnish

Method:

1. Add all the ingredients, except for the garnishes, to the cocktail shaker.
2. Shake until combined.
3. Add ice to the cocktail shaker and shake well.
4. Squirt chocolate sauce inside the glass
5. Strain the cocktail into the highball glass.
6. Garnish with chocolate chips.

BLUE LAGOON

Although it has a striking appearance, the Blue Lagoon cocktail is actually quite simple to make. Consisting of only three ingredients and with a classic flavour profile, this is a high-impact, low-risk recipe.

Equipment:

- Hurricane glass, filled with ice
- Bar spoon

Ingredients:

- 30 ml (1 fl oz) vodka
- 30 ml (1 fl oz) blue curaçao
- 120 ml (4 $\frac{1}{5}$ fl oz) lemonade
- Wedge of lemon, to garnish
- Sprig of mint, to garnish

Method:

1. Combine the vodka and blue curaçao in the hurricane glass.
2. Stir well until chilled.
3. Top with the lemonade and gently stir to combine.
4. Garnish with the lemon wedge and sprig of mint.

RUSSIAN SPRING PUNCH

"Punch" is the right word, as this cocktail features no fewer than three alcohols, including the famously heady champagne, with blackcurrant and lemon bringing the springtime flavours. Although it's called Russian Spring Punch, it was in fact invented in the 1980s in London, England.

Equipment:

- Cocktail shaker, filled with ice
- Strainer
- Highball glass, filled with cracked ice

Ingredients:

- 30 ml (1 fl oz) vodka
- 15 ml (½ fl oz) crème de cassis
- 15 ml (½ fl oz) lemon juice, freshly squeezed
- 20 ml (⅔ fl oz) simple syrup
- Champagne, to top
- Fresh raspberries, to garnish

Method:

1. Add the vodka, crème de cassis, lemon juice and simple syrup to the cocktail shaker.
2. Shake well to combine and chill.
3. Strain into the highball glass, over the cracked ice.
4. Top with champagne.
5. Garnish with fresh raspberries.

FUN FACTS

Perhaps the second most influential cocktail tome is *The Savoy Cocktail Book*, written by famous bartender Harry Craddock in 1930. Harry was one of the most acclaimed bartenders of the era and possibly the most famous head bartender at the Savoy Hotel's American Bar, in London. He is credited with inventing several well-known cocktails, including the Corpse Reviver No.1 and the White Lady, and is also often credited with the Martini's rise in popularity. He initially served under the Savoy American Bar's head bartender Ada Coleman. She herself is credited with the invention of the Hanky Panky for famed actor Sir Charles Hawtrey, who was a regular customer. He reportedly told her that he was tired and requested a drink with a little more "punch" in it. A keen recipe tinkerer, Coleman took this request seriously. The next time she saw Hawtrey, she offered him her newest invention, a mix of Fernet Branca, gin and vermouth. Hawtrey took a sip, and promptly and inadvertently named the drink, exclaiming, "By jove! Now that's the real hanky panky!"

BRAMBLE

Blackberries are a delicious seasonal fruit that provide a welcome tart bite to this gin cocktail. Dick Bradsell, the creator, was struck with inspiration while musing on the time he spent as a child picking blackberries and decided to create this recipe, which he described as a "British cocktail".

Equipment:

- Cocktail shaker, filled with ice
- Strainer
- Old-fashioned glass, filled with crushed ice

Ingredients:

- 60 ml (2 fl oz) gin
- 30 ml (1 fl oz) lemon juice
- 15 ml (½ fl oz) simple syrup
- 15 ml (½ fl oz) crème de mûre
- Blackberries or lemon slice, to garnish

Method:

1. Add the gin, lemon juice and simple syrup to the cocktail shaker.
2. Shake well, until chilled and combined.
3. Strain into the old-fashioned glass. Pour the crème de mûre on top of the cocktail to create the dramatic ombre effect.
4. Garnish with blackberries or, if not available, a lemon slice.

TOKYO BLOODY MARY

Traditionally, the Bloody Mary has been used as a hangover cure, probably because there is just enough spice, zing and vitamin content to get the worse-for-wear drinker going again. And if that doesn't do it, the dash of alcohol will!

Equipment:

- Cocktail shaker, filled with ice
- Strainer
- Highball glass, filled with ice

Ingredients:

- 50 ml (1 ¾ fl oz) sake
- 240 ml (8 ²/₅ fl oz) tomato juice
- 15 ml (½ fl oz) lemon juice
- 8 dashes of hot pepper sauce
- 8 dashes of Worcestershire sauce
- Pinch of celery salt
- Pinch of black pepper
- Celery stalk, to garnish

Method:

1. Combine all the ingredients, except the celery stalk, in the cocktail shaker.
2. Shake firmly and strain into the highball glass.
3. Garnish with the stick of celery.
4. For a classic Bloody Mary, replace the sake with vodka.

SINGAPORE SLING

The Singapore Sling is recognized as the invention of Ngiam Tong Boon, bartender at Long Bar in Raffles hotel, Singapore. He created a drink that looked like fruit juice, allowing women to enjoy a drink at the bar.

Equipment:

- Cocktail shaker, with a handful of ice
- Bar spoon
- Highball glass, filled with ice

Ingredients:

- 30 ml (1 fl oz) gin
- 30 ml (1 fl oz) cherry brandy
- 30 ml (1 fl oz) Bénédictine
- Dash of Angostura bitters
- 60 ml (2 fl oz) pineapple juice
- 30 ml (1 fl oz) lime juice
- Sparkling water, to top
- Segment of pineapple, to garnish

Method:

1. Add the gin, cherry brandy, Bénédictine and Angostura bitters to the cocktail shaker.
2. Shake well until chilled and combined.
3. Strain into the highball glass and stir in the pineapple juice and lime juice.
4. Top with sparkling water.
5. Garnish with a segment of pineapple.

LAST WORD

Hopefully, it has taken you many attempts to get to this page, having discovered crafts that you just cannot wait to create or recipes that you have to try instantly. With any luck, by now the pages of this book are covered with little splashes of citrus and the spine is broken open on the page with the cocktail that you never thought you'd like but can't get enough of – or your bar favourite that you can now recreate whenever the mood takes you.

Here's hoping that this book has become a party staple, living between liqueur bottles in your cocktail cabinet or balanced on top of your garnishes, ready to be whipped out when the next cocktail calls.

What was that? Is that cocktail hour calling already?!

COCKTAIL INDEX

Apple Pie 112
Aviation 98

Blue Lagoon 116
Bourbon Sour 64
Bramble 120

Caipirinha 62
Chocolate Mudslide 114
Classic Bourbon Smash 60
Corpse Reviver No.1 75
Cosmopolitan 46

Dark and Stormy 56
Diplomat 103
Dirty Banana 40

El Diablo 79
English Garden 86
Espresso Martini 44

French 75 110
Frozen Watermelon
    Margarita 107
Fuzzy Navel 42

Gin Daisy 96

Honey Bee 38

Incognito 80

Jerry Thomas's
    Whiskey Cobbler 78

Kir Royale 53
Kiwi Collins 97
Knickerbocker 82

Lemon Violet Shooter 54
Limoncello Thyme 70
Long Island Iced Tea 49
Lotus Blossom 59

Mai Tai 92
Manhattan 104
Margarita 50
Midnight Stinger 85
Mint Julep 73
Mojito 69

Negroni 55
Nobile 109

Original Planter's Punch 66

Piña Colada 88

Ramos Gin Fizz 76
Russian Spring Punch 118

Singapore Sling 124
Slippery Nipple 84
Snowball 106
Sparkling Citrus Punch 100
Squashed Frog 68
Summer Cup 102

The Last Word 94
Tokyo Bloody Mary 122

Zombie 90

Have you enjoyed this book?

If so, find us on Facebook at
Summersdale Publishers, on Twitter at
@Summersdale and on Instagram and TikTok at
@summersdalebooks and get in touch.

We'd love to hear from you!

www.summersdale.com

IMAGE CREDITS